TAPESTRY OF THE UNSPOKEN

A POETRY COLLECTION

Dr M. Elamaran

BlueRose ONE.com
Stories Matter
NewDelhi • London

BLUEROSE PUBLISHERS
India | U.K.

For permissions requests or inquiries regarding this publication, please contact:

BLUEROSE PUBLISHERS
www.BlueRoseONE.com
info@bluerosepublishers.com
+91 8882 898 898
+4407342408967

ISBN: 978-93-6783-663-7

Cover Design: Shubham
Typesetting: Sagar

First Edition: December 2024

Contents

NIGHT'S WHISPER

Whisper now, the night, what cloaks you in deep,
in your stillness, countless souls softly weep.
You cast your glimmers and dance in the dark,
nothing can silence the echoes that spark.

You weave shadows, a blanket of calm,
where ferocious hidden prowl, fierce as a hymn.
In your embrace, unseen marvels ignite,
before blinded souls, all things fade into the night.

Does brightness mute you, like your relatives below?
No one heeds their truth, as you reign from your glow.
Far from this realm, you govern the skies,
like our forebears, whose legacy never dies.

Like the sea, you have claimed the vast gloom,
who notices your strength when the moon catwalks through?
The world falls in love with the moon that it shows,
just as our minds chase the colours that please.

Your anger ignites the sky in a wild dance,
like a shattered dam, your brilliant radiance,
gliding like a legendary serpent,
enchanting the pure-hearted souls around.

Many see you as a mirror of Pandora,
in that mirror, countless beings find renewal.
True beauty isn't in colour but in how we see,
now, speak the night, what shrouds you in happy...

FORGOTTEN HEROES

When night descends and all find their rest,
they rise from dreams, no soft beds to nest.
In wakeup call, their gazes meet
with gentle smiles, old bonds restore.

After a day in stillness and numb,
they stretch, shake, and twist,
loosening limbs, they stand tall and proud,
descending from steed, cuddling with love.

Some call them icons, leaders of grace,
others see celebrities, in a timeless space,
many view them as artefacts
that highlight vintage delight.

Once a hero, now with no labels, no tags to define,
just names carved below, in a line so fine,
with stories of others, in detail entwined
in fancy fonts and bold.

Once or twice yearly, the people will come
to capture a perfect click with them.
With garlands of affection, they adorn for a while,
until the perfect moment, then leave with a smile.

The next day, some nameless will take garlands away,
or remain until it fades and decays.
But not all are graced with such fame and a shoot,
in the quiet of time, some remain resolute.

They wear the badge of symbols grand,
often they were a refuge, standing still
for lovers to hide, small animals,
and birds that sang in whispered hush.

Now echoes of time linger in the air,
yet the droppings of birds bring a pungent despair.
Nature alone bears the weight of their plight,
as we turn our backs, they get lost from sight.

Their lives weave the identity of our shared fate,
they who sacrificed for our comfort and peace.
Once the nation's heroes, they stood proud and tall,
now unseen in the rush, they silently fall.

As twilight ignites the heavens above,
they go still, revealing their essence and worth.
We consider who they truly are, and
we care for them, as they once cared for us.

LINEAGE

Who taught that little bird to weave
a wondrous nest among the leaves
from scraps and bits that nature gives!
Each day, I watch the tender dance
of mother and father, in happiness,
preparing for their future commence.

It all began with the season's birth.
In dusk's glow, a new journey unfolds.
A flock of birds colonized our forbidden tree,
where its roots hold history.

Rarely do I see a different kind of bird,
surprised, for this tree once intertwined
with many birds, as a vibrant gang,
now just one group of birds sing their song.

Leaves and birds, their blend so fine,
In shades of green, they interweave,
filling branches, a lively sight,
a knitting of love and fight.

Their lively gossip fills the air,
for days they bond with others so fair,
until the young ones find their mate,
In the shared branches, they celebrate.

I see these birds will not take a new mate;
once they find their love, it's their fate.
One may pass, but the other waits,
In life or death, their love always dwells.

At last, the birds crafted their homely nest,
guarding it well from others of their kind.
One smoky night, the mother laid three eggs,
as promise of hope, their life reborn in the cold.

Six couple built their homes, as a line drawn in the air,
and none were allowed to glance into another's lair.
When a stranger bird approached their tree,
one would swiftly shoo it away, who was near.

As time passed, the eggs began to break,
tiny lives emerged, a joyful wake.
Father and Mother flew to feed their young,
with watchful eyes, their love was sung.

Slowly, they peeked from their assigned space,
In moments alone, they moved to another's house.
They chirped and chattered, sharing their happiness,
while parents returned, their advice shattered their dreams.

Weeks rolled on, the adults grew bold,
endeavouring to walk out for their bond.
When parents came, they'd scold and say,
"Stay close to the nest, don't wander away."

"Enemies are on the prowl, danger is near,"
the mother warned, as she was fear.
"Is it wrong to visit the next nest?"
an adult bird inquired, in a quest.

The debate faded as they learned to soar,
parents taught them to hunt and explore.
Together they flew, then ventured apart,
finding their wings, following the heart.

Returning one day, the parents said,
"Now you can live your own style.
But value our blood, and hold them tight,
Never forsake our family's light."

"Among our kind, divisions are many,
seek friendships within, hold them closely.
This tree shelters six families, but only two are ours,
choose wisely your mate, beneath our stars."

The next dawn broke, the adult birds took flight,
parents prayed softly for their future bright...
"They should carry our Identity to next generation"
"You need to take them in right direction."

WAITING FOR WHY?

I was a tiny angel born in a sacred land.
I remember what Father once said,
"Tell everything to god, he's our last saviour,
whatever forbade will be accomplished."
I don't believe in god, but I believe my Father.
Upon arrival, I beheld;
A long line before divine's door.

This line stretched from tiny babes
to those who've seen a century pass.
As I stepped into the horde,
their eyes turned to me, filled with sorrow.
They embraced me, asking softly,
"What brings you to this place?"
When I sought to bring my horses home,
I was seized and rapped by cruel hands.
"Did you call upon God?" a woman smiled.
"All that happened within the temple,
Before the eyes of God," I replied.
I am no longer of this earth, except my body.
My parents weep, protesting for justice.
Yet, just as my prayers fell silent to God,
their justice fade into the void.

In silence, their eyes hung chill,
an old man approached, with love still.
He wrapped me close, his sorrow bled deep,
"This should not have been your fate," he wept.
but not a drop fell from his gaze.
"I should have not born, instead," I said.
"That's why I closed the doors of heaven,
Arrived just for an answer-
'Will you write the fate like this to your daughter?'"

A little child slipped from her mother's side,
crawling forth, with eyes so wide.
"Do you know," she whispered low,
"How they burned us, forties in a row?"
"Why did they do this?" I inquired.
"Because we dared to dream.
In our division, we toil and strive,
but born to serve, we barely survive."

No food, no home, no life to claim,
for those deemed voiceless, it's all the game.
Because we are untouchable by name.
When we rose for rights, we faced the flame,
the landlord's wrath, due to their cruel fame.
To heaven we ascended, but still I yearn,
with questions lingering, for answers I turn.
"Do you know what happens down below?
Did you divide us, make the pain grow?
If you see it all, why not descend,
To change our fate or defend?"

A girl beside me burst into laughter,
I turned to her, in caught off guard...
"Do you believe that God holds no power
overall that happens in our day?
Whatever we seek, the reply will be 'Karma'.
But is it true for every one's death?"
A voice from the crowd questioned aloud,
"I'm unsure, but an earthly saying."

"Was it Karma that I should meet my end
in the name of Honour Killing?
Look at that child, lost before birth,
a victim of lust–what's their worth?
Does the little child know the fate he bears?
Is it all tied to lives lived of previous birth?
See that boy, taken by fate's cruel accident,
another lost to illness, a sorrowful incident.
Many souls dawdle, seeking the 'WHY'.
We want answers for the reasons we die,
and we demand justice for lives torn apart,"
an old man's voice echoed, heavy with heart.

Power shapes all, it's plain to see,
those with wealth rewrite history.
"I find no difference from here to below,
perhaps it's our bodies that suffer the blow,
while here, it's the soul that bears the pain.
But Justice remains silent," a lady proclaimed.

Then suddenly, from the haze, a soul emerged.
We stood in a line, our hearts surged,
but it was just another girl who came forth,
all our gazes fixed–a moment of worth.

VENGAI-VAYAL

In our community stands an Eiffel treasure,
not as a symbol of romance, but life's true measure.
From dawn's first light to twilight's embrace,
the Elixir flows –our sustenance, our grace.

Once, our forebears journeyed far and wide,
in quest of this Elixir, their hearts as their guide.
Each time they unearthed its hidden delight,
a caste label loomed, casting shadows of plight.
To the fringes they ventured, burdened yet bold,
carrying treasures, their stories untold.

When our lineage faced the brink of despair,
the Elixir became our lifeline, our prayer.
Borders now shape our identity's core,
while latitude and longitude remain unsure.
Though our roots run deep in the soil where we reside,
outskirters we are, with our heritage as pride.

Each element we cherish bears our name:
the land we inhabit, the Elixir's sweet claim,
the temple we honour, all woven in fate –
the land, the Elixir, and God remain straight.
So sad, the land, the elixir and God doesn't know
that, they are labelled with our identity.

Unaware land uproots the Elixir
stored from the unseen place.
May be that's the reason, partition
yet to happen below the land.
Sometimes, being unseen is better than unaware,
but we are already living as unseen.

Sometimes, the unknown is a blessing in disguise,
for we are human, yet lost in the skies.
When taps run dry or candy melts unbidden,
they cast blame upon us, igniting the clash.
No reason exists for the rift that divides,
just a lack of the truth that in silence abides.

Until that fateful day arrives,
those who partake the Elixir realize the difference.
Difference is woven into our shared tale –
they labelled us as different.
But we are unknown that being 'different'
must drink and use elixir mixed with human feces.

Humanity, recorded painful histories
but failed to witness us with humanities.

UNKNOWN HUMAN

We, the unnamed souls,
escaped from divine's archetype.
Not storks nor deities, but flesh and blood,
we found our place upon this earth.

On that tragic day,
our first wail echoed,
a sound that has echoed through our days.
Gratefully, we embrace our mortality...

Outstretched hands left us in solitude,
fortified walls turned into horizons.
In boundless realms, we endured,
willingly treading reluctant soil.

Society dubbed us the third gender,
but who defines the first and second–
male and female, or the other way around?
Does anyone truly know who came first?

Stories shape our destiny,
even forget to capture our soul.
We may not bear the agony of birth,
but we have felt the anguish of rebirth.

People perceive us as the outliers,
but the true divergence lies within them.
While others chase after fleeting dreams,
we, the Others, possess nothing to lose.

As the world cloaks itself in conformity,
we stride boldly, unashamed of our truth.
Not all of us are beggars, jesters, or clowns;
the forbidden fruit, once savoured now belongs to us.

We are the phoenix, ignited by our identity,
and we shall rise anew –
this time, not with olden tales
but with our golden tales.

TOTEM'S SANCTUM

In the air, the sacred words disperse like poison's breath,
a towering sentinel looms, a warning in the sky's depth.
Figures stand, their legs a testament to battles fought,
colours once bright now fade, their vibrance all but caught.

In sounds of silence weave tales of yore,
the river of memory flows, recounting lore; "They were sisters,
Periamma and Chinnamma, protectors of the land.
In their sacrifice, they became divine, forever to stand."

Their temple rests at the city's edge,
where faith clashes with stigma, a struggle of wraiths.
To the left, the fields; to the right, the graves –
they stood strong for reserved souls.

A flickering flame gasps in the thorny embrace,
while tangled branches shield from celestial grace.
A crumbling tomb awaits its final descent,
rusty bells hang silent, their chimes long spent.

The road, once proud, now falters in rest,
where dizzying tridents hold still, with nest.
Sunken lamps of clay, buried in the sand,
a sign of donors, caste-marked by a hand.

Copious history ceases with ample trust:
"She is your grandmother; she is our trust.
Her power can cure deadly disease; all are allowed"
then said willowy priest, "but a woman must be married."

The entrance narrows, a passage of dread,
where darkness ignites the fears in our head.
To Chinnamma's shrine, he led with care,
lighting camphor, dispelling despair.

A half- expunged idol, three feet tall,
with sword in hand, it stands through it all.
Goat's blood and hen's flesh, offerings made,
smoke veils the path, as the living parade.

Food for all, after homage to kin,
emerging from branches where the Peepal begins.
No gates to confine, just faith and fear,
guarding the spirits and other deities near.

History and legend recount the tale of two sisters,
who lived and departed from this sacred soil.
Is it the spectral dread that birthed the Tomb and Tower,
or the bond of their love that lingers still?

Yet, countless emblems...

THEN AND NOW

In a realm where divinity is named,
a land of the Gods, through ages famed.
From empires to lords of the soil,
temples rose high, born of toil.
In the shadow of stone, all stood as one,
Yet upon completion, the balance was undone.

Ancient shrines, with stories retold,
olden myths woven into beliefs bold.
Festivals flourish, a dance with delight,
for the weary gods or the people's respite?
Tales weave on, like desires that soar,
endless as time, forever wanting more.

Each temple holds its own sacred norms,
with paths divided by human fate.
Not by divine hand, but by mortal decree,
Two names for the God, in duality.
Once the creator, human's creation,
In the evolution, it's a peculiar transformation.

Year-round, the ordination of the divine unfolds,
a spectacle as holy, yet commerce takes hold.
For blessings sought, the faithful align,
in queues that stretch, god-branded items.

Once, offerings were of flesh and of breath;
now the hundi spares both life and death.
Its size reflects the deity's might,
devotees offer coins, seeking light.
In gratitude–or in desperate to spare –
in currency of faith, we attempt to hire care.

Once, the gods roamed free,
now veiled in shadows, seeking harmony.
Today, their sayings seem lost in the fray –
not the fate of the gods, but of humans at play.
Where are we heading in this grand design?
In the rotation of time, what threads intertwine?

ABSURD REALITY

A flare of hope shines bright,
as we dreamed of escape from the night.
The darkness yields to a dawning light,
while the sun begins to rise, igniting the sight.
Our journey unfolds beneath a radiant glow,
as we unlock the temple, letting silence flow.
Old treasures gleam, polished by time,
with gentle touch whispers, "Our parents are nigh."

Hope blossoms, melting pearls into streams,
we find our way to a motel, it seems.
It's been ages since we've shared a meal,
with odd dishes served, surreal but real.
Until Venus stirs from her slumbering grace,
we're caught in a whirlwind, lost in the space.
A million words dance from past to the next,
as shadows entwine, the colours perplexed.

Wrinkles on her face mirror the moon's gentle glow,
I sense her thoughts tangled in a checklist's flow.
My wheels race faster than her mind's gentle chase,
stopping near a place where freedom finds grace.
When time's cruel alarm pulls my sister away,
into a home where shadows betray.
The wheels roll on, leaving me behind,
with a smile like a metaphor, bittersweet and blind.

My heart beats slow, yet echoes resound,
as I gaze at a poster, my thoughts unbound.
In that moment, I am reborn with a question's flame,
Is it the dog that won, or the cat in the film?

FUNERAL QUESTION

Flame ignites...
A candle's glow, a fervent blaze,
Illuminating shadows in a vibrant haze.
Light weeps for the dark,
as the sun begins to wane,
the voiceless moon descends, a silent refrain...
Yet you burn on,
burning brighter than ever before.

Did you hear the whispers from the skies?
Did you grasp the truth that never lies?
Then why do you drift like leaves in the breeze,
forsaking your love,
your faith reduced to a tease!
Your laughter, a mere echo,
And still you burn,
burning brighter than ever before.

Who is she, in this phantom of your dreams?
Why trade your life for her fleeting gleams?
You snatched away your father's pride,
and dimmed your mother's light inside.
Before the wounds of birth could mend,
you chose the sorrow that death could send...
Yet you burn on,
burning brighter than ever before.

You spoke of hell in her absence,
yet smile from the heavens–a curious dance.
You stood by me through fortune's embrace,
now my future aches in your empty space.
Can the ocean unveil its hidden lore?
Like the depths of my heart,
your thoughts I bore...
But you burn still,
burning brighter than ever before.

We placed my trust in you,
You placed yours in love,
Believe it or not, love finds another,
while you linger lost in the blur.
A desert may bloom into a field,
but death cannot yield what life concealed...
Yet here you are,
hibernating in flame,
glowing brighter than ever before!

You burn now...
You should have stayed to witness world's fire.
My friend, purity blooms with the dawn,
but the soul of life is born from the pyre!

SEARCHING

I'm searching, searching, searching
through and inside out,
I'm tumbling, stumbling, fading,
in this dance of my fault!
I'm shaping, shining, casting,
to mould your heart!

I know our souls must intertwine
before the world can tear us asunder.
The fragrance of love drifts gently
with the soft sigh of the breeze.
Faith is the art of navigating dreams–
where joy can both blossom and break!

You cannot feel the sun's sorrow
when you shine like the spark.
If longing is love, what then is trust?
Not every rivulet finds the ocean's crust,
Failures carve trails; others turn to dust.
You turned from my greeting–
and silenced my unvoiced pleas.

Oh, my Creator,
I now ponder your wisdom,
your principles spun from grace,
although humanity reads with clouded eyes.
The woods we call a den for beasts
are truly a haven for love and truth.
As a mortal, what can I yearn for?

DOES LIFE EXIST

In the stillness, breath's last whisper fades,
a lonely essence, where pride tumbles,
amidst the silence of fallen remains.
Did dreams betray the dawn of our chains?
The winds weave hymns, a prayerful refrain.

Scattered embers, lives once aglow,
from the dawn of hope, now shadows bestow.
Enflamed streams flow from wounds that seep,
as broken clouds weep, a river so deep,
nourishing the earth, our mother's eternal keep.

Echoes of prayers rise from the spires,
where love entwines with the weight of desires.
Joyful feathers flutter, yet souls lie still,
frozen in time, with a heart breath's chill.
In weapons at rest, yet the tension peaks thrill.

Innocent feet flee from their own ground,
searching for life where hope can be found.
A flame of triumph dances in glee,
over homes and lands, where sorrow runs free,
Owners and children in hunger disagree.

In every glimpse, missiles take flight,
claiming their victims, both day and night.
Drones of the scavenger confirm the end,
soulless spirits to judgment they send,
lost in the shadows, where no voices blend.

In shadows of steel, where the brave hearts dwell,
Some are bound in metal, while others bid farewell.
Forged in the fires of a relentless fight,
They wander as exiles, seeking the light.
But, tomorrow's harsh grip holds their dreams in cell.

Eden's land, once lush, now torn apart,
forbidden fruits plucked by a fractured heart.
Not by the devil, but by desire and thirst,
Earth, our sole haven, where life can aspire,
yet divided by power, we tread on the wire.

When we close our eyes, darkness descends,
Is it fleeting or forever, as the journey bends?
Each finds their path to the exit of being,
Survived love and peace stood linger, quietly seeing,
"Only we carve out a space for their freeing."

SHADES OF LOVE

In whispers long, the moon is deemed pure,
slowly my spirit ignites on nights obscure.
The cosmos hushes, waves dance in delight,
as shadows stretch deep into the night.

My feet wander where the people might roam,
but the sand clutches tight, refusing me home.
Stars of the bay, with their watchful gaze,
while the moon, envious, lingers in haze.
Yet still, my eyes seek the warmth of a crowd,
In the cloak of dark, I feel lost and bowed.

Yearning for love, a bond once so near,
now a ghost of connection, a whisper of fear.
Tradition's grip has loosened its hold,
as my restless gaze flits, searching for gold.
Alone in the silence, no faces to find,
yesterday's sorrows still linger, unkind.

My heart, it retreats, while my mind takes the lead,
even my shadow has chosen to heed.
Why crave a shadow if life feels so thin?
Am I truly alive, or just trapped within?

In the night's deep embrace, a shadow appears,
slithering softly, igniting my fears.
In inches closer; my anklet's song fades.
Could he be a seer, in the night's charades?
He shifts like a beast, majestic and bold,
while I bloom like a flower, in stories untold.

Is he divine, with a gaze that ignites,
reflecting my son's laughter, illuminating nights?
His voice, husky, weaves through the air,
"Shall we play?" he asks, with a fleshly stare.
If I refuse, how will I pay for my kin?
I bow like a martyr, surrendering within.

"I'll offer recompense, two thousand for tonight,
Be the queen in the soft moonlight."
Many have taken, in their violent spree,
But I feel no different, with human cruelty.

An empty vessel cradles our essence,
like a shrine that shelters the unseen.
The waiting moon sharpens its gaze,
while the restless waves lose their sheen,
in the shadow of a trust once keen.
Lust, he reshapes with yearning hands,
shielding me from prying stares,
as time drips slowly,
and pain spills from my eyes,
"Why has my husband left me in despair?"

The night surrenders to a pale blue hue,
I glimpse him, counting currency from his purse,
"There stands his wife, with children in view!"
The azure sky ignites to orange burst,
I whisper,
"Let this aching life fade with my virtue.
I perish daily to sustain this strife,
while you thrive by extinguishing the light!
We are not born, but sculpted,
by hands that wield such power.
I bear your sins and your grime,
be a guardian to your family, a faithful lover."

His eyes now blaze with sorrow's rain,
as tears cascade like a gentle stream.
My garment veils the flickering flame,
shadows cling to me, a haunting theme.
My feet find their way back home,
cleansing achieved with humble waters,
purity restored by divine grace.
A soul embraces me from behind,
whispering softly,
"You are the greatest mother in this world,
I love you, Amma."

A WITHERED BLOSSOM

In a parched expanse,
the sun shadows the landscape,
scotching fire turns waterbeds into relics,
a hollow of joy, in devoid of mirth.
My paradise crumbles,
as my cherub begins to fade...

Faith departs to illusion,
my convictions ignite in fire,
before my goddess is laid to rest.
In a heart of smoke, I glimpse a bloom,
its petals fluttering gently,
emerging from a shattered heart...

My paradise thrives on her fragrance,
countless bees seek to claim my rose,
still, my spirit shields it from their grasp.
I nurture it, whispering - you will
adorn my life, and my love
will restore the bounty I once knew.

Each dawn greets me with my rose,
a symbol of my affection.
My eyes twirl with her petals,
illustrating our dance of pollination!
Spencer's verses transform in motion,
a million words fall short of her essence...

As time flows with the day,
my love entwines with her grace...
There, I discover tender buds,
born anew in my garden,
My rose paves the way for my kin...
dryness yields to the embrace of spring!

New beginnings,
yet the same enduring love...
With a fresh name, a family!
One by one, my paradise becomes celestial,
some blooms white, others red...
where my heart bends toward bliss...

Milton's grand tale may falter,
when my paradise reclaims as mightier...
Each night, the moon weaves a lyrical serenade,
lulling my rose buds into slumber...
It sings a sweet ode just for us,
as our dreams gently shed their modesty!

My spirit sparkles with the dawn's embrace,
before the dewdrops twirl around us...
The purity of love births a multitude of joy,
the duality of flesh transforms into a magnetic force.
We name this existence eternal,
bound by the threads of life's permanence...

Until that fateful day arrives...
when I dare to open my eyes,
my rose has been taken by the divine!
with a note left behind,
"Earth is nothing but a fleeting kingdom,
our love endures; we do not!"

I behold my Eden, suffused with her fragrance,
her voice reverberates through every corner,
our buds have blossomed into full bloom...
The fantasy of love dances with the illusion of dreams,
I step out of the garden, where my rose
gently entangles my soul within its life...

THE DAY I WAITED ...

The Day I waited...
Fossils of fertile barrenness etched upon your visage,
eons of time yearning to share life with you...
Is this the insatiable desire of Eve?
Adam's heart, steadfast, refuses to yield...

Unnamed echoes swirl
around my ticking clock; with each heartbeat
new identities emerge from the shadows of loss...
The sun, a ravenous entity, awaits my arrival
while soaring falcons keep their watch - yet
my innocent heart seeks only you...

The moments I longed for your presence...
Rosebuds tear through the earth like precious ore.
Mechanical souls yearn for refuge
as lost birds wander without a name.
The jubilant sky captures a faded image,
an oxymoronic love sways in your direction...

The moments I waited for your return...
A bewitched breeze caresses my heart,
thunderous clouds illuminate my thoughts.
Miles traversed until the instant I behold you - yet
the enigmatic future births miraculous musings
drip by drip; I intoxicate myself with your blood.

The moment I searched for your presence...
Spring surrendered to summer's embrace,
oceans bowed to drought's demand...
Winds of migration matured into
devastating cyclones - and in their eye
you reigned with a mere glance...

The moment I waited for your presence...
Kama's parrot delivered a message
inscribed upon a scroll that read:
"Fides's promise ignites into a blaze...
Yama's thread guides a vessel -
awaiting my arrival."

The moment I felt your presence - resonating
"I am the same yesterday, today, and forever."
As the scent of belief began to climb,
past is destined for defeat and future is intended.
From the ashes of loss, we rise and reclaim,
with the choices we make, igniting the flame.
The past, a shadow, destined to fall,
while the future indented, who mastered the past.
From the ashes of loss, with courage you rise,
in the deeds of the present, your true strength lies.

The Day you said to me...

WAS IT ME?

Was it truly me ...over there?
Lying on the bed of stones?
Hot blood saturates the damp earth,
wheels spin, idling in anticipation.
A crowd circles, murmuring their thoughts,
while lonely flies stand as guards,
I see myself, breathless and cold.

The eagerness of the crowd morphs into whispers.
Some clutch my veins,
Some have taken hold of my chains.
Their harsh words push me away,
All in the rush to reach the office on time!
Was it me? I'm searching for my essence...
I see myself, devoid of sense, void of feeling...
Lying alone, down that forgotten path.

Is this a dream of mine?
Thoughts stretch and twist in agony.
I hear my mother's cries from outside,
I see my father's sorrow echoing within.
I feel a father's love shining above,
I sense my mother's warmth below.
Smiles and tears flash all around me...

An electric pulse grips me tight,
Voices whisper as the pulse fades away.
I see welcoming hands–
With a label; they named it an accident!
Some weep, some pray,
some search for what's lost,
others wait for the next arrival–
With the doctor's apology, my fate is sealed!

Waves of mourning crash against heaven's gates,
A gentle breeze tells the tale of love.
My wandering soul is ignited by a fierce cry,
my spirit resonates, a memory from the flesh.
Chanting mantras, defying the miraculous,
Who am I? A sailor, a soldier, or a writer?
The pain of birth–reborn! I awaken my senses.
Lost tranquillity found; I reclaim my humanity.

A heart of stone fractures with each tear that falls.
He liberates me from the shackles of souls.
I soar... I rush... to where my body lies.
I hear my parents' wails of despair,
I sense they are preparing to burn me–
What they believe is hibernation; they think I'm gone!
I stand beside them, yearning to speak–
But my words dissolve in the void of their grief...

I glimpse my history mirrored in the gazes of others,
Love cascading like tears that shimmer
in the glow of camphor's flame.
I reach for my mother, yet reality
fades into a faceless dream!
I roam around, urging, "Do not weep."
I shout and reach out; no one listens or senses
my emptiness, stripped of form and substance!

I witness my friends in sorrow,
A weight of flowers blossoms on me.
The air was thick with echoes of lament,
As the sun dips low, the moon weeps above.
A floral chariot nestled within these walls,
A charcoal flame flickered brightly–yet my
Father's hand holds me firmly,
trust gushing over me like a river.

Suddenly, heavenly doors open with–a golden ticket,
my earthly form reclaims its strength.
Worms transform into butterflies, soaring free.
My spirit seizes command of this vessel,
Like a sovereign claiming his realm.
My hands move with purpose, eyelids dance,
I felt my lungs inhale like wisps of smoke–
And my heart finds its rhythm at last!

A heart once shattered, now mends from sorrow.
Tears of despair morph into tears of joy.
All gaze at me in astonishment, proclaiming,
"A child of the divine; who triumphed over death."
Yet a whisper within me questioned–nothing is as it seems.
Consciousness entwined with the unconscious,
For every ending birth, a new beginning born,
in the essence of who we are...

The spirits that pursue us are eternal.
All embrace and celebrate as the priest intones
Mantras for immortality, casting sacred ash.
He declares, "It's your rebirth!"–I ponder,
If my birth is indeed a rebirth, then
What is my death? A re-death?
The cycle of life eludes comprehension.
The end of one birth is merely the start of another.
Breath resumes where it once ceased.

Petals cloaked me, discarded in a refuse bin–
And I whisper,
"It's poised for the next chapter of existence..."

SOME DAYS SOME NIGHT

Some days were like night,
sun floating around.
Some nights were like day,
stars twinkling above.
Someday, somewhere,
stars merge with the sun;
Soul finds its solace...

Some days were like red,
peace resting within.
Some nights were like white,
blood penetrates into.
Someday, somewhere,
blood merges with peace;
Soul finds its solace...

Some days were like fairy-tales,
truth crumbles down.
Some nights were like verity,
unicorn walk beneath.
Someday, somewhere,
truth merges with unicorns;
Soul finds its solace...

Some days were like illusion,
equality binds unity.
Some nights were like restorative,
existentialism blinds humanity.
Someday, somewhere,
equality merge with existentialism;
Soul finds its solace...

WHAT DEFINES YOUR BEAUTY?

What defines your beauty?
Is it the quietude you possess,
speaking volumes beyond mere words?
Are you perhaps unlettered,
setting you apart from the rest?
What defines your beauty?

Is there a shade of blue in your past?
a timeless smile that lingers,
a fleeting moment in the face of mortality?
Your gaze remains steadfast,
like a famished crown prowling the wild.
What defines your beauty?

Do you keep a tally of all things?
My spirit trembles at your honesty!
Even the mightiest idols fade
In the presence of your radiant essence.
Have you known love before?
For it is love that stirs the dormant soul.
What defines your beauty?

Is mercy absent from your heart?
You linger until I arrive,
and wait still as I depart.
Beauty is ephemeral,
Altogether, the beast within me falters
when thoughts of you arise.
What defines your beauty?

Why can't life rewind its course?
Yet, you reflect on humanity's plight.
The affluent become destitute,
while the lowly wear a crown of joy.
The spiritual journey feels excessive
before your pious soul.

Who am I in your eyes?
On my birthday, the deity whispered,
"Time is catching up with you."
My conscious fears awaken,
as your gentle hand waves, at last...
It may be last, yet I am not lost.
"Dear love,
I am but a thread in your tapestry,
all is yours for my next beginning..."

LOVE(ER) BATTLE

You made my heart break.
In that fracture, I found my refuge in you.
My celestial essence lost its clarity,
my sacred heart transformed into a hidden charity,
all with just a brush of your presence.

You made my heart dance fitfully,
and in that chaos, I wrestle with myself.
A once-mighty hand now falters,
a tempestuous mind torn asunder,
all because of your grasp.

You left me in a whirlwind of desire,
when my spirit discovered you...
The northern lights concealed unspoken words,
sweetness turned bitter in your thundering sight,
and in that storm, I find my haven in you.

You made my soul entwine with yours,
the wings of flies fluttered in perfect harmony,
cosmic sparks falling like fireflies' glow,
in the enchanting embrace of love,
we set the moon and sun aside.

Dreams morph into ideologies,
thoughts become fallacies,
your love is the sole basis.
The earth's rotation halts for us, yet
your shyness keeps me at a split.

Divine love sprinkles eternal existence,
but it pales next to our sacred bond.
Why do we deem temples as holy?
When the true sanctity lies within our souls,
where I stand as the sole priest.

With our love, history rewrites itself,
as Apollo dips his quill into our passion.
Your kiss could make Thais envious,
but who cares? Time marches on–
Before God can envy, let's recreate our paradise.

Let's rewrite the saga of a thousand-year conflict,
together, but without the tales of Greeks or Trojans.
Just you and me–where
the frontline transforms into our asylum–
Let the cycle of our love's battle commence,
an eternal war of the hearts.

AM I THE ONE, WHO STANDS BEFORE YOU

Am I the one, who stands before you?
With empty palms and an untouched heart,
am I the one who lingers here...?
Words devoid of meaning in a void world...

Am I the one, who stands before you?
I reign over my own existence–yet,
I wander like a tramp through life,
am I the one who lingers here...?

In my garden, blossoms thrive,
a tapestry of colours, one family–
Though born into kin, I walk alone,
am I the solitary one...?

I witness laughter echoing around,
I sense the whispers behind my avatar,
as I turn, a faceless shadow emerges,
from this place, I stand in solitude...

When my hopes manifest as truth,
you label it a mirage; are we
merely figments of our own creation?
And here I stand, all alone...

If I don't yearn for
the knowledge I consume, then why do I
exist as a human rather than a beast?
In this realm, I feel like a clone creature...

If I return to where we began,
then our coffins are but another womb–
If I seek the umbilical thread, they call me a spectre,
am I the one who lingers here...?

If joy is a diamond,
and smiles are mere sparkles–then
I am your coal, let life refine me through bother,
am I the only one who stands...?

If we are all equal in the eyes of the Divine,
then, why do divinities differ in form?
Equity is a puzzle, pieces scattered,
I stand alone in this division...

What truly nourishes life?
Is it the cultivation of wealth?
When we stash our riches away,
we bury our humanity in the earth...

Though the wings of failure may drag me down,
passionate feathers of success urge me onward...
I may be the one who stands before you,
but heed my spirit... I am not ready to yield!

IS THAT YOU?

Is that you?
Heart whispers...
Drifting clouds close our eyes
weeping blue shadows in sorrow.

Is that you?
Meaning echoes...
A mourning star dims in pale
concealing earth with a desolate touch.

Is that you?
Honest deceptions...
A searching spirit relinquished its grasp
darkened night ignites in brilliance.

Is that you?
Passionate yearning...
Halloween's trust entwined with reality
embracing a future that flees with the wild.

Is that me?
Corroding grin...
Whirling falsehoods masquerading as hope
days have ended, stepping into their graves.

Is that me within you?
Sanctified abyss...
Nestled trust lies in eternal rest
long-awaited wounds find their home.

Is that you once within me?
Smouldering grave...
A bridging womb becomes a haven for worm
morning prayers dissolve in dampened layers.

Is that me in my symbolic soul?
Paradoxical doubt, still.
Auroras inscribe destiny's tale,
banned rainbow arch opens to welcome fate...!

GENDER DISCRIMINATION

In the embrace of dawn's first light,
shadows linger, clutching tight.
From the moment we entered this sphere,
we were deemed ordinary, yet grew apart in fear.
Some stamp us as men,
others jest us as women,
in solemn whispers, we ponder the Divine.

We are Humanity!
But, we drift from our kin,
seeking our place in the rows of life,
yet left unrecognized in the columns of strife.

Atypical beings we are
in the asymmetric world.
Our gender questioned before
our identity; nevertheless, who cares?

Gazing eyes brim with desire,
tender deceptions scatter like fire.
To endure, we barter our souls,
we were everywhere...
Wandering on a speeding train,
sleeping under sailing sun,
dining with hands that know no gain...
nevermore, we remain silent,
because we are the Unseen!

DO NOT CLAIM THAT WE HAVE TIME TO SPARE

Do not claim we have time to spare,
life's melody echoes, a hunger laid bare.
Wings of flight cast shadows on every abode,
love intertwines, yet burdens each road.
Hate, a currency, passed from hand to hand;
art's price is steep, yet where do we stand?
A priceless spirit, cast aside in despair;
all we possess is to shield nature's care.
Yet nothing exists to save from our kind,
on one side, love nurtures a single soul's bind;
on the other, it sways the lives of the many.
Flames in our homes draw the eye,
while wildfires captivate the sky!
Is there no harmony for us to embrace?
What we covet in desire will vanish without trace.
Nature, crafted over eons, a masterpiece grand –
in every fleeting moment, we let it disband.
Where is the preservation that cradled our birth?
Not even fossils remain to mark our worth!
In every sacred ash, the remnants of fire,
we chant our prayers, but do we truly aspire?
We hope for salvation while shattering the divine;
humanity thrives in unity only when we cross the line.
In destruction and ruin, we find our reign...

LOST GENERATION

Someday, some memories –
somewhere they fade into shadows.
Some moments felt infinite,
somehow, they linger in the light.
Sunrise and sunset occasionally
evoke the forgotten world–where
butterfly hands seek
the treasure of the flying dragon!

Nights filled with tales, and that cradle
continue their last lullaby dance.
Countless times, twinkling stars descend
to play hide and seek behind a veil of ignorance.
An extended family never forgets
its joy and love, where
rain and river harmonized our
leisurely rhythms!

The cycling season never overlooked,
pedalling through our rice fields–where
our muddy land receives
its ceremonial feast on banana leaves.
In the dark screen over blue skies
reflected our school days.
One by one, they came and went, but
the memories remain forever...

Years together shift in phase and appearance,
where sun and moon seem to lease their light–
we locked our gates behind a façade,
which cried aloud for a virtual race!
Hopes and dreams smoke above,
while truth and love smuggle below.
One, two, three..., we lost our humanity and
labelled ourselves the last generation-
as our new identity.

RAVEN CARNIVAL

United ravens,
connected through calls,
discordant voices resonate,
gathered to share experiences.

A creeping sound rends the sky,
drifting clouds descend in fear.
Aimless wings, timing their flight,
joyfully soaring in hymn.

Foretelling the future, some ravens –
influencing fate, others –
manipulate with a magic wand,
sparking and smoking with iron beaks.

Chanting an alluring melody–
soaking their feathers in passion,
resounding with a distinct love,
in the embrace of night.

I gazed at one, perched beside my final resting place.
It probed and peered into my darkened eyes –
a fierce flame trapped in a narrow gaze,
warmth and fire, perspiring in my sight.

It flipped its beak, extending beyond the night.
How dreadful, I thought.
A flying raven circled above,
with a rhythm that made their wings flutter.

"What is happening?" I inquired.
"It's a raven carnival," the raven replied.
The darkness deepened,
only fiery eyes surrounded me.

Their forms blended into the night's embrace...
"What is the raven carnival?" I asked.
"It's a feast of sustenance," it answered.
I could no longer hear the fluttering sounds.

The creeping noise echoed flatly,
Perhaps a final summons for all, I mused...
"What's your special food?" I questioned.
It grinned, a devilish smile...

All advanced toward me.
It's you, the carnival.
I turned back, seeing myself lying there,
breathless...

YOU ARE NOT WHAT YOU'RE

You are not merely what you seem,
as years pretend in a fleeting dream.
Between the veils of truth and deceit,
I glimpse the essence where shadows meet.
From cosmic womb, an ascetic spirit takes flight,
dancing like stars, lost in the night!

Cyclic tides have lost their way,
time's embrace halts in disarray,
before our ecstasy unfolds.
The foam in the guardian's hand beholds
a century's crown for your brow,
why are you not what you are now?

The hide and seek of light and shade
concludes with your growth, a journey made.
Call forth Venus to wed Mars within,
to shun the gaze, let wisdom begin!

Beauty cloaks a hidden beast,
where night ignites desire, and day craves feast.
Spirituality bows to modest grace,
while saints embrace the modern pace–
In dreams, your heart finds its mate!

Like a root that breaks through the earth,
maturity blossoms by revealing its worth.
The chasm between you and your core
turns delusion into a bond evermore,
and you become whole, as I transform–
self emerges from inside out, a new norm!

With tears that fall like a mystic rain,
a vibrant arc weaves through joy and pain,
lifting life with its gentle curve,
as leaves drift down, reborn with verve.
Like a fallen angel, I'm soaring high,
In the embrace of your endless sky.

Idols remain silent, and so do you,
the fallacy of fate is not what it seems true.
Like a flame, your spirit ascends from below,
In all that you are, you're nothing, yet glow–
For that nothing holds a universe vast,
My life, once fallen, now free at last!

WOUNDED SOUL WOOING ALONE

A wounded spirit wanders alone,
ruptured dreams rise like the moon.
Greedy souls tread its paths anew,
shuffling shadows, mourning the view.

Home once cloaked in a veil of gray,
flames dance in the ashes as they play.
Prayers for peace in the air do swell,
while temples stand still like a closed shell.

We sought to break free from tedious mundane,
yet drifted apart in the search for love.
With the jingle of keys, our path turns bright,
and I slip through the gates, escaping the night.

The darkness lingered in quest of prey,
the moon wore a veil as a cover-up mask,
stars twinkled softly as if preparing to nap,
under the celestial crowd, my journey began.

To the temple we journeyed, seeking to cleanse,
the chime of the bells woke the forgotten tunes.
Tears fell like shards, a heart laid bare,
fragments of sorrow swung heavy in the air.

A gentle hand brushed away my grief,
with a voice that offered a glint of belief,
"Families are always with you," the priest softly spoke,
from woods of despair, the smoke of hope awoke.

In the spellbinding embrace of mantras,
our odyssey unfurled from the depths within;
as I grasped him close, visions crafting anew,
yet in the gaze beyond, he vanished from view.

Then, wheels rested by the roadside motel,
where weary souls dined, their struggles worn thin;
new-born plates paraded, each loss a refrain,
On the plate, my image mirrored my origin.

Strange food slipped past my lips,
miserable meat found a curious mix;
I sensed a wish for our absence to grow,
as I settled our dues for the care we'd forego.

The moon cast its glow, where shadows conspire,
wolves smiled with hungry look, in the night's choir;
On the solemn highway, our wheels carried light,
bearing the silence, where life is so tightly laid.

With the birds' gentle songs, dawn broke the night,
sunlight brushed the ocean as a canvas of light;
though darkness refuged within, and sealed over all,
as trees held their breath, in the stillness we fall.

A new day emerged, with echoes of yore,
wheels spun unyielding, a relentless roar;
the race ignited with the temple's wakeup ballad,
but my engine fell sick, beside of tomb's head.

I stepped into Hellenic trials, the door ajar,
where boatman stood, near Pandora's bizarre;
I handed him keys, bidding him to confine,
as my body was sealed, my soul joined the divine.

WHAT A HUMAN CAN BEAR

In the depths of shadows, we dwell.
A human's heart can't bear its swell,
In the dramatic furnace of the night,
some desires shatter like the kernel's thirst.

Is there a gauge for dreams to weave,
that crafts a fortress from reprieve!
Through myriad years, nature spins her thread,
to shape the morrow from what's ahead.

Even so tomorrow wears a mask of lies,
concealing truths beneath the skies.
In the narrow grip of fate's embrace,
each life emerges, for an ephemeral purpose.

Some are bound by sacred ties,
named and framed for future rise,
while others outlawed in disguise,
to bear and clench the weight of sin.

Do we tread our path, or merely trace
of echoes of a bygone race?
When good and evil dance as one,
the birth and death come undone.

The scriptures whisper of virtue's way,
a cosmic road where spirits sway,
to shape the muses, to seek the divine,
In the quest for eternity's design.

We follow the path laid by the aware,
bearing the badge before the bearer.
As pilgrims we march, seeking to rinse,
or ignite the flame that never ends.

THOU MY LOVE

A psychic breeze tales through my core,
chilling droplets cling to my attire,
O my beloved, how you dawdle evermore!
Years of memories cascade in a haunting choir...
Death's shadow dances, just before the door,
echoes of the past trace the steps I tread,
neither heaven nor earth can hold me in their hoard.
A parched longing shattered my youthful fallacies,
wishes feasted upon my grown-up dreams as fantasies,
trust, a transient mirage, left me misled.
Thou my love; eternally, you reign supreme,
shaping my heart upon your holy shrine;
Thou my love, in your hymn, I shine.
The relentless clock now stutters as hypnotized,
my restless heart slows, seeking solace near.
An ageless arrow slips from its bow, unleashed my soul,
the spectre of death nudges me with fear,
a weathered gaze implores your warm embrace,
with trembling hands reaching for your divine's hold...
A frozen fire grips my palm in its trace,
you forever find your place, in my verse.

THE WEAVER

Stripped spirits waiting around,
watchful weaver weaving about,
with different sizes and varieties.
Black some; Brown some; and white above,
each cloth sewed with its clan yarn, inside out,
Shape were still until rambling spirits popped into
versatile cloths find some stretch.
Each spirit suits its mortal cloths with likes and dislikes.
Enlightened spirits stepped out with peculiar name.
It's the weaver divided us as priced and priceless,
marked with emblem and yarn of the weaver.
It worked; awaited diversity sprang between cloths,
with tags and price!
Some were first, some were last, and many were lost.
Endorsed cloths clumped to exaggerate!
Dismissed cloths waited for approval.
Stripped spirits waiting around,
watchful weaver weaving about.

THE BIRTH OF VERSE

Light's vision hauls forth to reclaim,
while night's hands stir with restless flare.
Concrete bricks shimmer in hues bright,
a watchful eye of glimmers, yet is wrapped in night.
Silence unfurls its cloak all around,
as paths converge to a singular ground–
my aimless pen is poised for a journey grand,
with my door sealed tight, for a fortress, I've dreamed.

These four walls, like cages, confine my soul,
protruding its take-off, denying my goal.
A rusted clock bends its hands in distress,
In twisting and turning through shadows laid bare.
Crumpled pages exhale their last sigh,
with half-formed thoughts that dawdle and die.

Above, a dim light flickers and sways,
while we breathe deep in the gloom of our days.
On the edge of a wooden, unyielding floor,
haunted solace whispers, urging for more.
It stirs the past, seeking a fresh start,
filtering through life's routine, a weary heart.

Books on the shelf, once dormant, now awaken,
slowly stirring my thoughts like Poseidon.
I hear their deep howls, their cries intertwine,
thoughts echo hollow, in both yours and mine.
Their weeping tears pierce through my skin,
"Don't cast us aside, for without you, we're thin!

Embrace us, hold us, let our souls blend,
in this lament, let our spirits mend."
They mourned and they wept, till I drew them near,
as birds whispered softly, their songs crystal clear.

Aromatic hymns danced on the air,
toasting our senses–a fragrant affair.
Inch by inch, light reclaimed the night;
as darkness retreated, yielding to bright.
Inexpressible thoughts blossomed within me;
together, we wove them, setting them free.

Before dawn's arrival, the carriage lay bare;
in your hands, my pen– we promise to share.

RHYTHM TO WESTWIND

In contrast to the tempest of the monsoon,
you are a tender drizzle in a parched land,
a vibrant sapling dancing in my barren musings.
Like a scarecrow, you stand sentinel, observing from afar.
Your pure essence weaves together the diverse artistry;
like withering leaves fall from a fading root,
I find solace in the way you grace the ground beneath you.
The whispering breeze carries the fragrance
of your unvoiced thoughts,
while the echoes of life linger beneath
your deep, resonant breath.
Solid stone revives ancient images,
each one a testament to struggles engraved in the yoke of time.
We seek refuge in these remnants to navigate
your hardscape of memories that lie ahead.
You are the rainbow that twists and turns
through our aspirations,
and though you may appear colourless,
does it truly matter?
To a heart that aches and yearns for a brighter tomorrow...
The realm of the divine reaches its conclusion
when your fury stirs the air.
Still, your soft smile sends ripples
through the murky waters of selfish souls.
Oh, my westwind...
The sun guides the moon,
darkness gives way to light,
and if destiny leads our love to falter,
life on this earth becomes fragile and fleeting.

RAYS OF LIGHT FALLS ON WORLD

Golden beams of autumn light surge upon this realm;
the hands of darkness clutch them tightly in the chill.
Life's arrival gifted us the ordinary–yet,
as we flourish, we find ourselves set apart.
Some call them Men,
others impishly name them Wo-men,
though all are solemnly cradled in divine hands.

We are the Human!
Distanced from Humanity,
chosen for our deeds.
We began our quest, searching in neat rows,
but remain unmarked in the columns of existence.
Are we destined to reshape the past,
or manipulate what lies ahead?
The present slips away, fading into memory!

Do we embody humanity within our human forms?
Tomorrow crumbles into dust,
when eyes and hearts consumed by covet.
Striving hopes, endure and elope;
a magical mantra gossips its truth.

What are we below the guise of perception,
resting on a speeding train,
slumbering beneath a wandering sun,
feasting with hands ablaze?
We may appear rough on the outside,
yet we are delicate within.
We are the human!

Cast out from the womb of our mother
to the embrace of the earth,
erased from the living, sewing
bound in a lifeless narrative for stealing.

Like lions in a circus,
we are confined within the bounds of imagination.
Like refugees in a forsaken land,
we inhabit our own territory.
No day mirrors the one before,
no dawn resembles the dreams we hold.

To possess greater strength than yesterday,
we are burning the fuel of tomorrow for today!

LONG SAID, MOON IS A SIGN OF PURITY!

In ages past, the moon was deemed a symbol of purity,
though here I stand, thriving in its absence,
a shadowed existence, unbound by its glow.

The universe murmurs softly,
as playful waves gamble, teasing the sandy shore.
In the heart of night, my feet crave the spark,
warm grains of sand cradle my weary soles,
while distant stars clutch at my spirit.
The envious moon longs for my gaze,
but my eyes remain steadfast,
yearning for dawn's embrace.

Love's depths have long been abandoned.
Once-vibrant bonds have shed its pride,
traditional ties now loosen their hold.
Trauma has unravelled its tight embrace–
the feathered sky observes in tranquil silence,
as the effervescent night bows low...
Yet still, I find no trace of light.

An aimless night seeks the void ahead,
like a child, it waits for the thrill of unwrapping a gift.
Yesterday's wounds lie buried beneath the surface,
not every day does the child offer its affection.
Some nights, I must rest with an empty heart,
though love never truly leaves my side,
still, I find no sign of light.

More than my soul, I place my faith in shadows,
never have I glimpsed them in the dark.
Only in the depths of night do shadows seep into my being;
that's when I await my spark.
Though light may blind my weary eyes,
it is the sustenance my senses crave.
My gaze reaches out for the nourishment to endure.

Still, no sign glimpse of brightness appears.
One by one, stars and the moon have tasted my appearance,
leaving nothing for me to share.
The rhythmic breeze emerges, weaving its tune,
while hunger wobbles, extending its song.
The hands of hunger stretch out for the day–
Am I forever destined to seek the light?

ITS ROTTEN MEADOW

It's land, once vibrant, now decayed,
a tempest looms, its fury displayed.
Snowflakes ignite as they dance through the air,
while sun and moon weave their luminous snare.

Humble seas morph into forests dense,
where creatures lie still, in a tomb's recompense.
Ghostly vessels drift, with shadows aboard,
slumbering giants awaken, though ignored.

Metropolises cloaked in wealth and despair,
after villages shattered, survival laid bare.
Capitals twirl like the auroras above,
echoes of howls in the fields that we love.

A pyre of humanity smoulders in shame,
trees wheeze their lament, as if calling a name.
Roots tremble and twist, seeking solace in ground,
while famished spirits cling to branches for liberation.

Food, once sacred, now trapped in a shell,
as farms turn to tokens, a protest to tell.
Blooms and green blades find their place in the halls,
while grains and their seeds hold jubilant calls.

Fields transform into briny expanse,
oceans fossilized in a timeless dance.
Metaphorical tides swirl in the sand,
as creatures lie still, like statues they stand.

Humans evolve into something less whole,
with circuits of thought, yet a hollowed-out soul.
Senses programmed for slumber and feast,
as oxygen flows for a city's cruel beast.

Divinity wanes, its wonders now lost,
nature's elements claim the throne at great cost.
Crossing the borders, the lines of our race,
where heedless souls drift in a featherless space.

Children confined, in their chambers they wait,
till maturity metamorphosis, though sealed is their fate.
Playgrounds now boxed, where laughter once soared,
slowly they seek what it means to be adored.

On the brink of our being, we teeter and sway,
centuries squandered for fleeting display.
When truth wears a mask, and doubts entwine,
life in a comatose dance, a warning divine.

Factories and industries, a lifetime confined,
gardens and fields, in history interlocked.
Future generations, lessons to glean,
as fading humanity finds solace in dreams.

Minerals and acids, remnants of toil,
unearthing treasures from the rich, fertile soil.
An electronic passage morphs into green streams,
beneath currencies lie buried, lost in our schemes.

Bees and birds, reshaped by design,
flora and fauna, in human hands confined.
Synthetic springs rise from the depths of despair,
life's cycle reborn through the unity we share.

Once we stood firm, our rights to defend,
though we may perish, our legacy bends.
Our essence transformed into ore for the young,
learning from errors, a new song to be sung.

We may forfeit our faces, yet not our core,
identity remains, a rich, vibrant lore.
Meaning can flourish, if kindness prevails;
For men and women, the love, must not fail.

IT'S AROUND SIXTEEN

In the dusk of sixteen,
the heavens wear a shroud, no stars to gleam,
a fierce wind twirls the clouds in a waltz,
whispering trees sing a sorrowful tune,
the moment our eyes first intertwined...

Raindrops fell like a gentle stream, where
your beauty struck like lightning's embrace,
while others hid from the tempest's rage,
I stood soaked, engulfed by love's tide,
the instant I caught sight of you...

In solitude, life lays a lavish spread,
a solitary heart blooms with timeless grace,
am I adrift in a your mirage?
My spirit weaves dreams with the fabric of fantasy,
the second I stumbled upon you.

Your stare was a journey,
your lips tasted the breeze,
your hands crafted a symphony,
I cursed the skies–why, human?
why not just raindrops...

As clouds drift away with you,
I sought stars in the morning light,
your thoughts seethe like embers within,
my father inquired, "Are you alright?"
In silence, my heart yearned for your touch.

Night and day, I tread your path,
an ecstasy star illuminating your visage,
melodies that flow, echoing your spirit,
my feet defy the earth,
still my soul reaches for your return.

Will I ever behold you again?
A minefield of memories detonates within,
thoughts layered in sorrow,
like an avalanche, your essence finds its place,
In dreams, a beautiful day forever lost in trance!

IT WAS NOTHING

It was nothing...
as I stepped out,
with a vision blurred,
thoughts dipped in sorrow.
It was void,
as I stepped inside

Souls whisper secrets,
in cryptic languages,
when bodies inscribed in
ancient texts of wisdom.
It was empty,
as I stepped inside.

Fields lay barren
where grains should flourish, bricks rise,
like leaves dance in sadness,
soul weave a haunting melody...
It was empty,
as I stepped inside

I glimpse a heart ablaze beneath,
while ashes twist and swirl above.
Flesh once living morphs to silicon,
and thoughts of circuits rules the realm...
It was empty,
as I stepped inside...

A sacred space turned into a trench
with humanity standing on the front lines.
Innocence shattered, children weep,
crimson rivers stain the sacred ground.
It was empty
as I stepped inside.

Traditions and hierarchies spiral into chaos,
Love and faith teeter on the brink,
I see facades traded like currency
as souls embark on a quest for self...
It was empty
as I stepped inside.

I witness the ravagers all around–
Land divided by borders, states torn apart,
inequity spreads like wildfire, cloaked in power.
It was empty,
as I stepped inside.

It was empty
As I stepped inside...
I lost my essence, I pondered deeply
Who am I...?
Did I grant them freedom and rights?
Or have I landed on the parallel world...?

The Divine turned away, posing a riddle!

IS THAT OF ALL I HAVE IN THIS BIRTH

Is that of all I have in this birth, I sung,
If that of some left me in blue, what I brought.
Morning flocks flip natures' cheek,
unfolding blurry stretches; with folds and fades,
fantasies of hopes rinse and raise from dimpling dew.
Alas! Budding river cuddles like an infant unwilling towards the unknown,
shadows of untouched souls rush to find its womb...
Shrunken meadows recollect from oozing dream,
pregnant buds avail breaks, walking in delivery line,
one by one, the sand mine open, and bud turns feathered,
Inch by inch, red-cap soldiers marches for food!
Blending fire bleeds in east, peeping the ball in higher,
lengthened light waits in queue near the building square.
Lazy leaves ignite its lurking colours to sign a contract
with lousy, buzzing bees for love making,
restless bees begin its orchestra with romantic symphony.
In the deep beneath the locked walls,
breathing souls open its blistering eyes to hire their soul
for one more day; life born again in faith.

I DON'T REMEMBER WHERE I STARTED

I cannot recall the origin of my journey,
a radiant sun stirring joy in every soul,
the moon's gentle murmur beckons dreams of slumber.
A soft embrace of leaves begins a melody of wings,
frozen remnants warm in the tender dance of dew and dawn,
like a fairy's curls, the river glides through meadows.
Snow-capped peaks shiver, as echoes tremble,
a spirit entwined within the human form...

Light intertwines, casting rainbows anew,
a new-born star, vibrant in its hues.
Wings flutter, showering the air with whispers,
furry legs scurry, seeking refuge from the storm!
A modest bud greets the kiss of a breeze,
time after time, the sun climbs the mountain's spine–
like step by step, like a reluctant cloud,
it drifts, casting shadows over the city, a curse unkind.
Yet filament light weaves the promise of tomorrow...

Wheels that bear humanity–
begin to erase the tales of yore,
from the slumber of nature, like a chronic ailment,
it coughs upward–within homes; outwardly!
Zebra crossings stretch to the mountain's embrace–

Where dying cries shatter the celestial veil with each chop!
In every timber's fall, the human spirit ascends;
the beauty of existence lies in the nakedness of creation.
Desolate roads teem with hollow hearts–
They race for no purpose but their own!

The weary sun drifts toward the clamor of towers–
where the rhythm slows in the haze of smoke;
alarms wail for sustenance;
humanity bends toward the mechanical.
Some wear smiles behind tears, others weep before deceit.

A life of despair leaps from generation to generation!
The slowed tempo finds its sanctuary in the end!
Light from above, guiding souls' home,
in the hands of existence, like shattered shells.
The belief rises anew, burying its past beneath the pains...

Above, divines all together having their supper,
Oh, their idol statue divided in tranquillity below!
I shiver at the memory of the chill with this sight;
Father, adorned in silvery grace, transforms slowly.
"Is that you, dear God?" I ask, a smile blooming.

He cradles me to slumber, snaking tales of paradise.
In dreams, like a nurturing angel, he enfolds me,
not in fallen heaven, but in the stolen Eden!
With love eternal, he guides me to a timeless peace.

In this realm, I alone savour nature's splendour.
While the world slumbers, some eyes remain vigilant,
reflecting on beginning...

CLIFF'S BREEZE CLIMBS MY SOUL

The breeze upon the cliff ascends,
chilling sweat, a frozen blend.
Oh, my love, though you are near,
years of memories, crystal clear.
Death walks softly by my side,
as shadows linger where dreams abide.
A past half-burned, yet it revives,
in the will of love, where our spirit thrives.
Not in hell, nor on this earth,
"Do we rise again, giving love rebirth?"
The thirst for love stole my youth,
while lustful feasts clouded my faith.
Trust, a fleeting tale, deceived my heart,
Thou, my love, who tore us apart,
sailing away to the eternal tide,
leaving me alone, with nowhere to hide.
The clock ticks on, a stuttering breath,
while my restless heart dances with death.
In search of solace, it slows its race,
While knocking echoes in this empty space.
Future awaits, a regal embrace,
wrinkled eyes long for your grace.
My lone hand craves to clasp your own,
in frozen flames, where my soul has grown.
The awaited day greets the icy night,
but, through our love, we find the light,
bound together in an endless embrace,
inside the gate's heaven, we find our place.